Home for Christmas

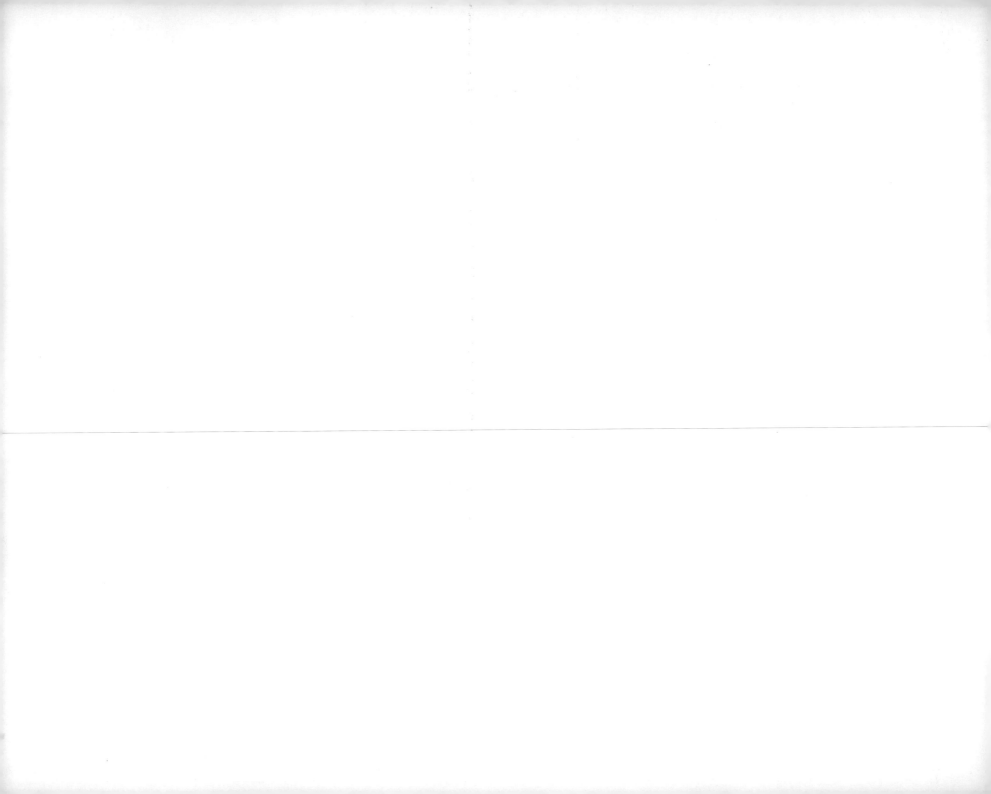

HOME FOR CHRISTMAS
Cards, Messages and Legends of the Great War

Peter T. Scott

Tom Donovan

London

First published in 1993 by

Tom Donovan Publishing Ltd.
52 Willow Road
Hampstead
London NW3 1TP

ISBN: 1-871085-17-9

Designed and typeset by Tom Donovan Publishing Ltd.

Printed by the Bath Press, Bath

Contents

Acknowledgements

The majority of the cards reproduced in this album come from the collections of the author and the publisher. Others have been generously loaned by John Bodsworth and others who kindly made their collections available to us. We are most grateful to Peter Liddle for his guidance and assistance during the author's most enjoyable and fruitful visit to the Liddle Collection at the University of Leeds, and to Peter Halsey of the London Library; the staff of the St Bride Printing Library and David Cohen for their interest and help.

P.T.S. & T.D., August 1993

Publisher's Note

Most of the cards reproduced here have been reduced in size by approximately 20-25% in order to accomodate them. Most of them were originally standard postcard size, or thereabouts, although a few were appreciably larger (eg *Plate 50*) or smaller (eg *Plates 35-38*).

References

Unpublished sources

The papers of the following officers and men are housed in the Liddle Collection, Leeds University Library, and extracts appear here by kind permission of the Keeper, Peter H. Liddle: Captain Sir William Baynes, Bt, MC, Coldstream Guards; Captain L.W. Jardine, Royal West Surrey Regiment; Captain T.C. Osmond, RAMC; Private W.M. Peto, ASC; Major W.A.A. Phillips, MBE, 24th Punjabis; Lieut.-Colonel B.H. Puckle, DSO, 57th Battalion, MGC; Private D.F. Stone, HAC; Private A. Douglas Wills, 78th Battalion, CEF.

The letters and diaries of Lieut.-Colonel H.M. Pryce-Jones, CB, CVO, DSO, MC, form part of the Scott/Broadsword collection and extracts appear here by kind permission of Alan Pryce-Jones.

Extracts from the following War Diaries housed at the Public Record Office, Kew, appear by kind permission of the Keeper of Public Records: WO 95/25 Adjutant-General, GHQ; WO 95/81 Director of Army Printing and Stationery Services, GHQ; WO 95/1488 HQ 11th Inf. Bde.; WO 95/2541 A & Q Staff, HQ 38th Div.

Published sources

Anon. The Unofficial History of the Military Forwarding Services Overseas 1914-1919. Privately Printed, 1927.

Bidder (Maj. H.F.). Three Chevrons. by "Orex". Bodley Head, 1919.

Boisseau (H.E.). The Prudential Staff and the Great War. Prudential Assurance, 1938.

Bridges (Lieut.-General Sir Tom). Alarms and Excursions. Longmans, 1938.

Brown (Malcolm) and Seaton (Shirley). Christmas Truce. Leo Cooper, 1984.

Bruckshaw (Horace). The Diaries of Private Horace Bruckshaw 1915-1916. Ed. Martin Middlebrook. Scolar Press, 1979.

Buday (George). The History of the Christmas Card. Rockliff Publishing, 1954.

Burgoyne (G.A.). The Burgoyne Diaries. Thomas Harmsworth, 1985.

Chandos (Lord). From Peace to War: A Study in Contrast 1857-1918. Bodley, 1968.

Charteris (Br.-General John). Field-Marshal Earl Haig. Cassell, 1929.

- At G.H.Q. Cassell, 1931

Condell (Diana). 'A gift for Christmas: the story of Princess Mary's Gift Fund 1914' in Imperial War Museum Review, No. 4 (1989), 69-78.

Daniel (F.W.). The Field Censor Systems of the Armies of the British Empire 1914-1918: Unit Allocations. Vol. I. Burnham on Crouch, 1984.

Elton (Lord). Among Others. Collins, 1938.

Ewart (Captain Wilfrid). Scots Guard. Rich and Cowan, 1934.

Gordon (H.). The Unreturning Army: A Field Gunner in Flanders 1917-18. Dent, 1967

Gray (Frank). The Confessions of a Private. Blackwell, Oxford, 1920.

Griffith (Ll.Wyn). Up to Mametz. Faber and Faber, 1931.

Hatton (S.F.) The Yarn of a Yeoman. Hutchinson, [1930].

Hay (Ian). The Willing Horse. Hodder and Stoughton, 1921.

History of the Great War based on Official documents: Military Operations: France and Belgium: 1916. [Vol.II] Compiled by Captain Wilfrid Miles. Macmillan, 1938.

- 1917. [Vol. I]. Compiled by Captain Cyril Falls. Macmillan, 1940.

- 1918. [Vol. I]. Compiled by Br.-General Sir James E. Edmonds. Macmillan, 1935.

Hitchcock (Captain F.C.). "Stand To": A Diary of the Trenches 1915-1918. Hurst and Blackett, 1937.

Jack (Br.-General J.L.). General Jack's Diary 1914-1918. Ed. John Terraine. E&S, 1964.

Kennedy (Alistair) and Crabb (George). The Postal History of the British Army in World War I, before and after, 1903 to 1929. Ewell, 1977.

[Luard (Miss K.E.)] Diary of a Nursing Sister on the Western Front 1914-1915. Blackwood, 1915.

MacDonagh (Michael). In London During the Great War: The Diary of a Journalist. Eyre and Spottiswoode, 1935.

McLean (Ruari). Joseph Cundall: A Victorian Publisher. Private Libraries Association, Pinner, 1976.

Moran (Lord). The Anatomy of Courage. Constable, 1945.

Murray (Sir Evelyn). The Post Office. Putnam, 1927.

Pimlott (J.A.R.). The Englishman's Christmas: A Social History. Harvester Press, 1978.

Proud (E.B.) History of [the] British Army Postal Service. Vol. II: 1903-1927. [Brighton], c. 1981.

Robinson (Howard). Britain's Post Office. OUP, 1953.

Sams (Lt.-Col. H.A.). The Post Office of India in the Great War. Times, Bombay, 1922.

Sandes (Major E.E.C.). In Kut and Captivity with the 6th Indian Div. Murray, 1919.

Scott (Peter T.). 'Christmas Day 1914', in War Monthly, No. 60 (1978), 18-20.

- 'Christmas in Plugstreet', in Stand To!, No. 12 (1984), 23-27.

Sorley (Charles Hamilton). The Letters of Charles Sorley. CUP, 1919.

Sulzbach (Herbert). With the German Guns: Four Years on the Western Front 1914-1918. Leo Cooper, 1973.

Terraine (John). 'Christmas 1914, and after', in History Today, Vol. 29, No. 12 (1979), 781-789.

Williamson (Henry). 'The Christmas Truce', in History of the First World War, Vol. 2, No. 4 (c.1970), 553-556.

The Bookseller. 1914-1918.

The Illustrated London News. 1914-1918.

The Stationery Trades Journal. 1913-1919.

The Stationery World. 1913-1919.

The Times. 1913-1918.

The War Illustrated. 1914-1918.

Introduction

Christmas 1913 marked the 70th anniversary of the first commercially produced Christmas card. In November 1843 John Callcott Horsley, later a knighted Royal Academician, had produced a festive design at the suggestion of his friend Henry Cole, later one of the creators of the Great Exhibition and also knighted. The cards were printed from a lithographic stone, hand-coloured and "possibly not more that 1,000" were sold at the considerable sum of one shilling each by Joseph Cundall, Cole's associate and entrepreneurial publisher.

Cundall is not known to have published any further cards himself, but others took up the idea and slowly at first and then at an ever increasing pace the Christmas card gained complete acceptance as an essential ingredient of Victorian Christmas celebrations and in so doing created a wholly new trade that by 1913 numbered over forty Christmas card publishers and wholesalers in London alone and employed many thousands in production and distribution. For example, in December 1913 the newly opened Croydon factory of A. Mason and Co. ("A Leading British Christmas Card Publisher") employed over 300 workers.

The Penny Post, introduced in 1840, mechanised envelope manufacture, the repeal of the duty on paper in 1861, the appearance of the postcard in 1870 with its special half-penny rate that also applied to unsealed greetings cards, more economic printing techniques and cheap imports (particularly from Germany), all combined to bring the Christmas card within the means of all. Indeed, by 1883 *The Times* was able to record that while the "poor may indulge... to the extent of one half-penny - nay, even less, we believe - the rich, if so minded, may expend five guineas on a single card." The additional volume of mail generated by the sale of Christmas cards was startling and Henry Cole recorded that by the 1880s 11½ million extra letters were being handled in Christmas week. By 1913 the normal weekly delivery of 14½ million letters increased to well over 25 million immediately before Christmas and in addition over 50 million letters were sent to overseas destinations.

The British army was certainly not immune to the inexorable rise of the Christmas card phenomenon. Specially designed cards were a commonplace for many regiments by the early 1900s and military publishers and printers, such as Gale and Polden in Aldershot, competed with commercial printers and the growing numbers of specialist publishers to supply suitable cards, mostly to the officers mess, for units at home and abroad. There were also occasional civilian cards with military themes and colourful uniforms that were doubtless sent by soldiers to their families and friends, quite possibly because the military cards tended to be very restrained designs. For example, *Plates 1* and *2* show

Plate 1

the Gale and Polden 1913 card for the 2nd Coldstream Guards with just the regimental badge in gilt and a ribbon tie on the cover and tiny sepia

H.B.D.H. Opening Meet, November 1st, 1913.

Plate 2   *Plate 3*

drawings of Coldstream uniforms from 1650 to 1913 within. However, with the development of improved half-tone printing came an increasing use of photographs in cards, such as that shown in *Plate 3* from the 1913 card of the Household Brigade Draghounds at Victoria Barracks, Windsor.

1914

By August 1914 Britain's Christmas card publishers and wholesalers were well advanced with their plans to ensure that a fresh range of colourful expressions of seasonal goodwill would fill the shops the following December. The trade papers had been carrying special reviews of the new cards since April. Raphael Tuck and Sons (holders of a warrant of appointment from the German Emperor) were offering 5,000 entirely new designs, including the "Trés Chic," "Silken Plumage" and particularly the "Pot-Pourri" series that gave off "a dainty perfume." C.W. Faulkner and Company had over 1,000 designs on offer, of which "by far the largest proportion... are produced on their own premises... only a very small proportion being imported from the Continent."

The outbreak of war caused immediate disruption to Christmas card marketing. However, "Business as usual," that swiftly coined slogan of wartime commerce for "everyone except the idle and the fighting man," was, as we shall see, reassuring to all except those who did import their wares from Germany, where the Kaiser was confidently telling his departing army: "You will be home before the leaves have fallen from the trees."

Among the men of the British Expeditionary Force (BEF) landing in France there was an equally strong belief, though less portentously expressed, that they would soon be on the journey home, having first assisted their French allies in gaining a quick and decisive victory over the German army. The families of the BEF translated this quiet conviction into the hope that their menfolk would be "Home for Christmas," while the flood of volunteers responding to Lord Kitchener's call for men to join his New Army greatly feared that the war would be ended before they could get to it: that it would be "All over by Christmas."

According to Lord Moran, a front line medical officer, the British Regular Army of 1914 drew its strength from its acceptance of "the religion of the Regiment - that only the Regiment matters; a faith which made our professional army... in German words, 'a perfect thing apart.'" From this army was drawn the BEF, later described by Sir Basil Liddell Hart as "the most highly trained striking force of any country - a rapier among scythes." The planning of the BEF had been meticulous and the provision of a small but efficient postal service acknowledged the value of regular contact with family and friends in maintaining morale.

The personnel of the Royal Engineers (Special Reserve) Postal Section came from the staff of the Post Office and at the outbreak of war it had an authorised establishment of 10 officers and 290 men, sufficient to serve the six divisions of the BEF. The Director of the Army Postal Service (APS) in France was Lieut.-Colonel William Price, CMG, a veteran of the postal service in the Boer War and one of the very few senior staff officers at GHQ to retain his appointment throughout the Great War.

"Ian Hay" (actually Major - later Major-General - J.H. Beith, MC, novelist and contemporary chronicler of Kitchener's New Army with his book *The First Hundred Thousand*) declared that the "Postal service of the British Expeditionary Force was one of the unadvertised marvels of the War" and, except for outline histories for postmark collectors, its

work certainly seems to have gone largely unrecorded.

The APS was operating just as soon as the BEF landed and adapted quickly to the rapidly changing circumstances during the war of movement that characterised much of the early fighting on the Western Front. For example, the 2/Coldstream Guards (4th (Gds.) Bde., 2nd Div.)

Plate 4: Men of the APS serving with the Indian Corps in France, Christmas 1914. Sacks of mail are piled behind them.

reached its billets at Vadencourt on 16th August and had to wait only until the 19th for their first letters, most of which had been posted in Britain between 12th and 14th August. The battalion continued to receive mail during the Retreat from Mons, though four bags were accidentally left by the roadside "and now I presume the Germans are smoking my cigarettes" grumbled Captain Harry Pryce-Jones as he wrote to his wife, Vere, on 4th September, asking for fresh supplies. This letter did not reach London until 17th September, by which date the battalion was settled down to its first period of trench warfare along the River Aisne, and the day on which they took delivery of ten bags of mail posted in Britain between 29th August and 4th September. Thereafter, letters came in "driblets each day," and as Captain Pryce-Jones told his wife: "The only thing we have to look forward to is our mail and I cannot tell you how grateful I am to have your delightful and precious letters." Vere Pryce-Jones had a bonanza delivery of her own on 2nd October when she and her family received a total of 25 letters, postcards and parcels from her husband.

The homeward bound mail of front line troops was collected by each unit's Post Orderly at a set time each day (in the case of the 2/Coldstream on the Aisne it was 7pm) and delivered to the Field Post Office attached to the HQ of the Brigade with which the unit was serving. From here it went to the Field Post Office with the HQ of the divisional supply train and thence to the base Post Office where it was sorted into about a dozen regional groups. This soon proved inadequate and FPOs were instructed to sort homeward mail into 27 Provincial Centres for Britain.

Initially, postage was payable on letters (1d per oz.) and postcards (½d) from the BEF, but this was waived on 28th August on the grounds that stamps were unobtainable on active service; thereafter homeward bound letters were carried free up to 4 ozs. Letters from Britain to the fighting fronts went at 1d per oz. throughout the war, even when the domestic penny rate went up to 1½d in June 1918.

For front line officers with the right connections there was an unofficial but perfectly legitimate method for circumventing the Army Postal Service by using the War Office King's Messengers (a title to which, strictly speaking, they were not entitled) and this became especially attractive when average delivery times to and from home by APS were around 10 days. By comparison, when Vere Pryce-Jones was given the opportunity of sending a letter to her husband via a King's Messenger, Lieutenant Lord Ilchester, on 1st October, it was delivered to Harry Pryce-Jones in his billet on the Aisne during the evening of 3rd October: "It was a wonderful feeling to think you had written it only two days previously."

When, towards the end of 1914, Captain Pryce-Jones was appointed Deputy Assistant Adjutant General at the headquarters of the Inspector General of Communications at Abbeville he discovered that the use of King's Messengers by Staff Officers for private mail was an official perquisite of the job. Letters to France were sealed in an envelope addressed to the officer concerned and then placed inside another envelope marked for delivery to the Private Secretary of the Secretary of the War Office. At the War Office the outer envelope was removed and the letters sorted: "The War Office make up two bags, one goes to Sir John French [at GHQ] and one comes here [Abbeville]. Each is given to a separate messenger who calls at the WO at 7.45 each day (Sunday included) for these bags - our messenger arrives here about 4pm by motor from Boulogne." (Even this system was sometimes circumvented by the simple expedient of delivering the letters by hand to the Messenger's London home!) Letters home bore a 1d stamp and the censor stamp (usually the officer's own) and were carried in the Messenger's pocket to be posted in London: "he leaves here at 11.30 each morning, arriving in London at 8 or 9pm".

Kindly disposed King's Messengers would always carry small parcels in either direction and, as a matter of course, took the staff newspapers "of every description, so we see them on the same day that they are published! Very luxurious!" One Messenger, Captain Hon. Lancelot Lowther (later Earl of Lonsdale), not only took them newspapers "by the dozen" but also "usually some pheasants and wonderful cheese each week." Luxury indeed.

And then there was the Military Forwarding Service, formed at the instigation of the War Office in September 1914 under the command of Captain E.C. Simpson, MC. Initially it handled private parcels too heavy for the APS, all "comforts" for general distribution to the BEF, and the free issue of newspapers to the troops. Later it grew substantially as its responsibilities were enlarged, but it too remained an "unadvertised marvel" of the BEF at war. Its central role in the celebration of the first wartime Christmas will be described later.

At the front the steady approach of Christmas, if remembered at all, went largely unremarked, the troops having more pressing matters to attend to. However, on the Home Front both charitable and commercial forces were at work from early autumn ensuring that the festive season would not go uncelebrated on the Western Front. Alongside the many regimental "Comforts" funds that had been working since the outbreak of war there were now numerous other funds, many of which had aims specific to the Christmas season. The most prominent of these was Princess Mary's Gift Fund launched on 14th October with the final aim of supplying everyone "wearing the King's uniform on Christmas Day" with a gift. It was to comprise an embossed brass box with contents that varied, but that for smokers included a pipe, tobacco, twenty cigarettes monogrammed with Princess Mary's cipher, a small photograph of the Princess and a Christmas card. See *Plate 5*.

Plate 5

Another Charity was the National Relief Fund, founded by the Prince of Wales with an appeal only three days after the outbreak of war. The Fund issued a specially commissioned patriotic National Christmas Card, *Defenders of the Empire*, designed by the noted military artist Harry Payne, printed by Tucks and issued in two styles (one mounted on khaki coloured board, the other on antique white board; see *Colour Plate 1*) to retail at 6d each, the entire profit going to the Fund.

The first letters urging a boycott of German manufactured Christmas cards and other printed goods had appeared in the press by the end of August and went hand-in-hand with other anti-German import campaigns that led to such products as Kruschen Salts being advertised with ringing declarations as to their "All British" manufacture.

A number of card manufacturers banded together in double quick time under the slogan "Beware of Printed in Germany" to warn the public not to buy any card coming from Germany, Bavaria, Saxony, or Austria, pointing out that 70 per cent of the trade was in German hands.

Sir Adolph Tuck was equally quick to point out that all these German cards had been "imported long before the war was declared and... paid for by, and is the property of British traders" and that they might therefore be "readily purchased by the patriotic public, who will thus truly protect British interests." However, this commonsense approach - bearing in mind that Tucks had always imported a proportion of their own stock from Germany - failed to impress the public, or the stationery trade whose papers reported the boycott in the same terms as the battles in France: "British v. German Cards; Desperate Battle Raging; Thorny Problems; The Public Must Decide; Trade Attitude."

Initially, the public decided by simply not buying cards at all. In Liverpool card sales were reported to have declined from 5 million in 1913 to 750,000 in 1914 and the demand for "private" Christmas cards (where the name of the sender was printed in the card) fell away to the point where the President of the Newsagents,' Booksellers' and Stationers' National Union had to appeal to the public to send such cards "as usual this year," pointing out that "this trade is quite a British industry."

Slowly, the momentum of Christmas sales of all kinds built up at home and Michael Macdonagh, a *Times* journalist, observed:

"There have been the customary crowds of shoppers in the West End. The Strand, Piccadilly, Regent Street and Oxford Street were as thronged as I have ever seen them at Christmas-time. And, as usual, people were buying gifts for others as well as things for themselves. In the suburbs the butchers' shops were bulging with beef and mutton; the poulterers' with geese and turkeys; the grocers' with wine, spirits and beer; the fruiterers' with apples and oranges. Yes, supplies are abundant; prices were only a little in advance of those last year; and money seemed to be plentiful. As for the 'Compliments of the Season,' friends were moved, because of the War, to shake hands with heartier vigour, and wish each other a Merry Christmas in sincerely and more gladsome voices."

While Dennison's ("London's most interesting shop") were busy offering everything from tinsel cord and gummed ribbon to decorated crepe paper and fireproof festoons, other manufacturers were quick to produce gifts suitable for the "Man in Khaki." *The Times* noted "Sombre piles of woollen jackets, cardigans, fur-lined coats... socks... sleeping sacks, and all the thousand things that practical ingenuity can suggest as likely to be of use for active service." They considered the tinder-lighter the most useful gift of the season: "Many of these... with their natty little plaited 'rope' and striker, have found their way into the trenches and have proved a wonderful boon, and their lasting power and the small space they take up in the pocket are great recommendations."

Gifts and cards flowed across the Channel to the BEF and the Post Office reported that in "the six days preceding December 12th... 250,000 parcels were addressed to the troops at the front and in the following week there were over 200,000 more and 2½ million letters."

The increase in the volume of mail being handled by the APS necessitated the use of additional road transport, including motor lorries and horse-drawn transport impressed from the streets of Britain and often still displaying their civilian liveries. Harry Pryce-Jones's London home was in Buckingham Palace Road, a little way from Gorringes the outfitters, something of which he was forcibly reminded one bleak day in mid-December as he walked across the courtyard outside his Abbeville office, feeling very homesick: "When I realized I saw a Frederick Gorringe Buckingham Palace Road dogcart... filling up with mailbags. Quite unconsciously I was carried away, even before I had read the name on the cart."

For those lucky enough to be stationed in towns like Abbeville there was at least some chance of buying gifts, cards and calendars, even if the choice was very limited ("the toyshops here are wretched places"), but for front line troops there was simply no choice at all. They sent their Christmas greetings in letters and tore advertisements from magazines and newspapers indicating the presents their families should buy for themselves since the soldier was not there to do it himself.

As Christmas drew closer so the quantities of "comforts for the troops" increased, ranging from private gifts - one of Vere Pryce-Jones's aunts sent the 2/Coldstream 50 lbs of tobacco and 100 pipes - to the distribution of the Princess Mary gifts that were described as "causing more work to the staff than several big battles!!" Captain James Jack of the 1/Cameronians (19th Bde., 6th Div.) recorded: "The number of

Reproduction of an original sketch made by an Officer at the Front.

Plate 6: This commercially produced postcard reflects the importance to the troops of contact with Home and Family through correspondence.

Christmas letters, plum puddings, mince pies, cakes, tobacco, socks, mufflers, wool vests, and electric torches received by us... was really immense. My parcels include oatcakes and shortbread from my Brother besides pate de foie gras..."

Plate 7

Each soldier in France was to be given a ration of ½lb of plum pudding on Christmas Day and, in the first major test of its efficiency, every single ration was transported by the Military Forwarding Service:

"There were thousands of puddings all packed in tins in cases - and Father Christmas in charge was dressed in Khaki - surely a strange dress for a messenger of peace! He travelled in one of the trucks on top of the puddings with a candle from his Xmas tree to pierce the gloom.

At Rouen the various trucks were sorted out and despatched with their precious loads - should we call it ammunition - to the various destinations.

On Xmas Eve at each Railhead or Depot was an animated scene as the supply officer of each unit presented his chit for so many plum puddings - which reached every man in and out of the line as a reminder of times of peace in the past and as a hope for peace in the future."

The King and Queen sent a Christmas card to each soldier, sailor and nurse. See *Plate 7*. In the BEF it was "kept a great secret and nobody knows about it," but every attempt was made to ensure that no soldier went without the Royal greetings when the card was officially distributed on Christmas Eve. Two staff officers drove from Abbeville to Amiens to deliver cards to four wounded British Soldiers reported to be in a French hospital there, only to discover that they had already been moved, one of them to Rouen where Captain H.F. Bidder of the Sussex Regiment was commanding a draft on its way to the front:

"We marched down to the station on a perfect day, and waited there three hours. A clear sky, a tendency to frost, an afternoon wintry sun, bright on Rouen spires - it was very inspiriting. At the station the King and Queen's Christmas card was dealt out to us. Its direct simplicity went straight home. I know it is very much appreciated, for I have been censoring the men's letters this morning. There is a personal note about it that I find very touching."

Very few Christmas cards were produced for the troops to send home in 1914, there simply hadn't been the time or the inclination to design and print them. But Lieut.-General Sir Henry Rawlinson, commanding

Plate 8

IV Corps, did find the time to produce two designs of his own. One, "from Lady Rawlinson and The friends of the 4th Corps," was sent to everyone serving in the Corps (see *Plate 8*), and the other, "Hooray for the King," was for them to send to family and friends.

Plate 9: Soldiers of the London Rifle Brigade in trenches near Ploegsteert Wood, Christmas 1914.

Christmas Day 1914 on the Western Front is now the *only* Christmas of the Great War to be remembered, the reason being it was the day on which peace was declared: spontaneously, very briefly, and wholly unofficially, at various points along the British held front line. And it is precisely because it was unsanctioned by higher authority that there are few first-hand accounts of the truce and the fraternisation in the official records. One exception is this eyewitness report by Captain J.D.M. Beckett, commanding C Company, 1/Hampshire (11th Bde., 4th Div.), who were holding the front line just north of Le Gheer on the eastern edge of Ploegsteert Wood. It is published here in book-form for the first time:

"Report on proceedings to the front of Hampshire Regt Trench on Christmas Day: The night 24/25 was particularly free from sniping to our front, the enemy were singing Christmas carols and their national songs. About 10am on Christmas morning I was making a sketch of the trench under cover of fog when I saw several of the enemy approaching from the trench north of our T piece [trench]. I shouted out for them to halt, not firing as the enemy was without arms; this was complied with and I sent forward a patrol to state that they must approach no nearer and return to their trench or I should open fire. The enemy then returned to their trench.

Soon after more of the enemy were seen approaching from their main trench to the east of our position; these men were also halted and a patrol sent forward. As the patrol seemed unable to induce the enemy to return to their trenches and more were seen approaching I went forward and asked to see an officer. An under-officer came forward, but I failed to make him understand me; an interpreter however was soon produced and the enemy asked that there should be no shooting as it was Christmas Day and that they should be allowed to bury their dead, of which there were a considerable number, a short way in front of their trench. This request I granted as by this time considerable numbers were walking about outside their trenches.

A spot was indicated just by their foremost dead which I informed them if they passed I should be compelled to open fire and that after dusk I should open fire on anyone outside the trench. The enemy agreed to these conditions and kept to them throughout the day. Towards evening what looked like a staff officer appeared and ordered all back to the trenches which order was immediately complied with.

To our right front a gathering of some two to three hundred men of both sides took place, the men exchanging gifts, handing over [the] enemy's dead from near our trenches and even exchanging rifles. Throughout the day I kept the garrison of my trench from contact with the enemy, the men not being allowed out of the trench on the enemy's side."

Beckett then went on to identify the German regiments (133rd and 134th Regiments, 40th (4th Saxon) Division) and to describe the design and layout of the German trenches. It is perhaps because of its intelligence content and the fact that Beckett did not allow his men to fraternise with the enemy that his report survives today.

These acts of truce and fraternisation, that were "after all only strictly in accordance with human nature," have taken on an extraordinary legend-like existence and it is sometimes very difficult to remember that there were numerous places along the front line where there was no truce, no fraternisation and precious little by way of the Christmas spirit. These are extracts from the diary of Captain G.A. Burgoyne of the

2/R. Irish Rifles (7th Bde., 3rd Div.) near Kemmel:

"December 24th. The Battalion marched into the trenches, my company going into Reserve in a big derelict farm... all the living rooms full of hay, on which we sleep, and we found a few plates, soup tureen, cups, etc., and there's an odd cane chair or so; but not so much in the way of firing, and as all the windows are broken, its cold and draughty.

Our Yule Log is an old paraffin tin, perforated and filled with live coals: not a bad substitute as it's freezing now.

Xmas Day. ... A Merry Xmas! A slowly dying fire (and no fuel to replenish it) in a big room, the windows broken, a frozen midden pond outside and a heavy fog. Inside a litter of hay and newspapers, a big deal table, and on the mantel the usual glass covered statue of the Virgin and Child; dinner is laid, bully beef, stew and potatoes, ration biscuit, a few sweets and tea minus even tinned milk. The food was so poor that Becher refused to wash before dinner and so came to the festive board, as he said, 'dirty.' We drank to 'Absent friends' in rum and water, but out of the four of us, no one could give the toast. So we all stood up and stared very fiercely out of the windows and gulped it down.

Our Christmas Dinner was very much a frost, as I fear we were all contrasting our present with the past, or what we hope will be the future.

At 9pm I took my company into the Support farm, a Sergeant Arnott, who had a piece of plum pudding (which had been sent out to him) left, gave me a tiny piece, as I said I must have one bit of plum pudding on this day."

Captain Jack and the 1/Cameronians were in the front line at Houplines:

"Christmas Day. The weather has suddenly changed. Hard frost replaces the rain, rendering digging easier, the parapets firmer, and the blocking of drains which run into the trenches possible.

Notwithstanding the Day, the ordinary round of duties, sniping and shelling is carried out."

It was not until 13th January that Jack recorded that there were "extraordinary stories of unofficial Christmas truces with the enemy" and having stated "There was no truce on the front of my battalion" went on to speculate: "It is interesting to visualise the close of a campaign owing to the opposing armies - neither of them defeated - having become too friendly to continue the fight."

On the other side of no-man's-land Herbert Sulzbach was serving with the 77th Field Artillery Regiment (24th (2nd Saxon) Division) on

Plate 10: A soldier of the LRB with officers and men of the German 40th (4th Saxon) Division in no-man's-land, Christmas day 1914.

Christmas Eve:

"It's snowing, a proper Christmas atmosphere... and at 5 there's a church parade; a big garage has been transformed into a church. On each side of the altar a fine Christmas tree is bright with candles, and 'palms' have been put up all round the walls... It is all so solemn and uplifting that you had tears in your eyes before you heard the strains of *Silent Night*. We were all much moved and felt quite melancholy, each taken up with his own thoughts of home... The Regiment gave me a most splendid Christmas present: I was promoted to the rank of *Gefreiter*, lance-bombardier, and it did me good to be picked out like this after so short a time."

Behind the British lines on Christmas Day Sister K.E. Luard was aboard an ambulance train on its way to collect wounded:

"Sharp white frost, fog becoming denser as we get nearer Belgium. A howling mob of reinforcements stormed the train for smokes. We threw out every cigarette, pipe, pair of socks, mits, hankies, pencils we had left; it was like feeding chickens, but of course we hadn't nearly enough.

Every one on the train has had a card from the King and Queen in a special envelope with the Royal Arms in red on it... that is something to keep, isn't it?

7 p.m. - Loaded up at Merville and now on the way back; not many badly wounded but a great many minor medicals, crocked up, nothing much to be done for them. We may have to fill up at Hazebrouck, which will interrupt the very festive Xmas dinner the French Staff are getting ready for us. ...This lot of patients had Xmas dinner in their Clearing Hospitals to-day, and the King's Xmas card, and they will get Princess Mary's present. Here they had oranges and bananas, and hot chicken broth directly they got in.

12 Midnight. - ... We had a very festive Xmas dinner, going to the wards which were in charge of nursing orderlies between the courses. Soup, turkey, peas, mince pie, plum pudding, chocolate, champagne, absinthe, and coffee."

Meanwhile, Lieut.-Colonel Tom Bridges, Head of the British Mission with the undefeated remnant of the Belgian army holding the tiny unoccupied corner of their country on the Channel coast, was looking forward to a festive round of golf:

"My brother Edward, who... was now in a New Army battalion of his old regiment, the South Staffords... came out and spent Christmas with me and had his first glimpse of the war. There was a well-known golf course at Lombartzyde on which the Belgian championship had been played the year before, so after a good lunch, washed down by Nuits St. Georges, Ted and I who used to have very well-contested matches, set out on Christmas Day to try and play a round. We found the club-maker's house, now a strong-point in the front line, still partly standing, and plenty of clubs and balls lying about. Thus equipped we managed to play a good match of seven or eight holes, though the number of bunkers had become rather excessive. We had to hurry on one or two greens owing to the unsporting conduct of snipers and spent half an hour in a pot bunker guarding the sixth hole. ... The match ended all square and one to play, which we decided to renounce as the Germans seemed to be getting cross."

At home the officers and men of the New Army celebrated their Christmas confident that the war was certainly going to continue long enough for them to reach it. Lieutenant Charles Hamilton Sorley was with the 7/Suffolks (35th Bde., 12th Div.) at Shorncliffe:

"We had a very swinging Christmas... We gave the men a good church (plenty of loud hymns), a good dinner (plenty of beer), and the rest of the day was spent in sleep."

The 7/Suffolks landed at Boulogne on 30th May 1915 and Sorley, considered by John Masefield to be the most promising of all the soldier poets, was killed in action at Loos on 13th October 1915; he has no known grave.

1915

So, it was not all over by Christmas. Some of the truces lingered on into the New Year, but GHQ issued an order forbidding any "recurrence of such conduct" and as units in both front lines were relieved in the normal course of trench routine the troglodyte war reasserted itself.

On 30th December the Routine Orders issued by GHQ included the following "Notice" that amounted to an advertisement on behalf of the company that printed the King and Queen's Christmas card:

"Messrs. W. & D. Downey, Photographers, 57 Ebury Street, London, S.W., have designed and manufactured special pocket cases to hold the Xmas cards sent by Their Majesties the King and Queen to the troops. These cases, samples of which have been sent to Corps Head Quarters, can be obtained from Messrs. W. & D. Downey, price 1/-".

The staff of the newly formed First Army gathered at Lillers on New Year's Eve for dinner with their Commander, General Sir Douglas Haig:

"There was no formality and no rejoicing. It was a quiet friendly meal. On the lips of all was the question: 'What has the New Year in store for us?' Haig gave the reply: 'We can but hope and go forward to meet what the future may hold with faith and without fear.'"

In fact, in Churchill's words, "1915 was fated to be disastrous to the cause of the Allies and the whole world." For the British the year on the Western Front was a catalogue of deadly place names that marked a stubbornly static siege warfare: Neuve Chapelle, the Second Battle of Ypres (the first use of poison gas on the Western Front), Aubers Ridge, Festubert and Loos. The news from elsewhere was no better: the landings on the Gallipoli Peninsula found the Turkish as resolute in defence as the Germans in France, while Mesopotamia, East Africa, Palestine and Salonika swallowed men and *matériel* without appreciable gain.

In France the distribution of the accumulation of 1914 Christmas gifts and comforts continued well into the New Year. Private W.M. Peto of the A.S.C. had landed in France in late January 1915 and it was not until

11th March that he noted:

"I have had a tobacco pouch given me as a Christmas present from Princess Mary's Fund. A lot of cigarette lighters were also distributed, as well as combs, mufflers, mittens, knives, etc."

The seasons turned and as autumn slid into winter the possibility of a second wartime Christmas became a certainty. Based on the lessons and experience of the previous year various festive plans were being made, but one at least was being cancelled. The King and Queen had been reluctantly compelled to abandon their intention of giving Christmas Cards to their troops as they had in 1914 when the distribution had been confined to France and Flanders. This year the King and Queen had wanted to give cards to all the troops on active service "in almost all quarters of the globe." The authorities had been forced to point out that "it would be impossible to undertake the transport and distribution of the cards" and the scheme was unwillingly dropped, never to be revived.

predominant note in this season's issues... which on the whole do credit to British design and craftsmanship." Tucks offered their usual wide range of cards and Gale and Polden had "representations of old and new types in the Navy and the Army, treated with originality and freedom."

More formations and units took the opportunity of producing and selling their own cards. Sir Henry Rawlinson once again designed a card for his IV Corps (see *Plate 11*), before leaving to take temporary command of the First Army in the aftermath of Haig succeeding Sir John French as Commander-in-Chief. At XI Corps the Assistant Quartermaster General, Lieut.-Colonel A.F.U. Green, produced a pencil sketch for the Corps Christmas card (see *Plate 12*), but at the 3rd Division they looked outside the BEF and obtained a design from the comic artist W. Heath Robinson (illustrated on dustjacket). These cards were printed in Britain, a luxury not available to Sergeant B.G. Tomkins of the Royal Marine Light Infantry who designed the card for the Royal Naval Division on Gallipoli. Bearing the imprint "Produced in the Field" it was duplicated on ordinary foolscap writing paper and folded to make four sides (see *Plate 13*).

Plate 11

At home the Christmas card trade had recovered from the disasters of the previous year and *The Times* recorded that patriotism was "the

Plate 12

On the home front the comforts funds and other charities once again made particular efforts for Christmastide. *The Daily News* Christmas Pudding Fund made Collections in the music halls and theatres and the YMCA organised "a scheme whereby Londoners may 'adopt' a lonely soldier either for Christmas Day or for the full period of his Christmas leave."

Plate 13

As to presents for the serving soldier in 1915 there was "a big demand for tinned things, soup and meat extracts, cakes, plum puddings and the like, and very many people have made a point of including in the parcel one of the little solid-fuel stoves." While it was true that experience had shown that "the fewer impedimenta those going on active service receive the better" this certainly did not apply to the ever buoyant demand for tobacco and "smokers requisites": "A novel and not too expensive present that had attracted many buyers is a leather cigarette case designed to fold very flat for the pocket. It holds 30 or more cigarettes and the proper thing to do is to send it to your fighting man full." For the ladies at home the obvious gifts were, apparently, a diary "now that everyone is keeping one," and a subscription to a lending library!

Special efforts were to be made to bring cheer to those in hospital. In France the Red Cross made an "issue of stores appropriate to the season": 10,500 tons of sweets, 1 ton of Brazil nuts, 1 ton of filberts, 2½ tons of almonds, 1 ton of walnuts, 1 ton of chestnuts, 3 tons of dried fruit, 10,000 boxes of crackers and 20,000 Christmas cards. Having been evacuated from Gallipoli Private Horace Bruckshaw of the Plymouth Battalion, RMLI, spent Christmas in a Convalescent Camp on Lemnos where the Red Cross reached him with "a neat little gift of writing paper, cigarettes, handkerchief, toothbrush, matches, etc. Of course we dined as usual but by way of a treat we finished up with plum pudding."

Once again the flow of mail to the Western Front built up as Christmas approached and "during the ten days previous to 25th December 1915 over 210,000 bags of letters and parcels were carried across the Channel." The traffic to Britain was just as great and in one week of that December "there were posted in the B.E.F. Army post offices 5,160,713 letters and 52,477 parcels."

There were to be no truces for the BEF this year, of course, the order forbidding them would see to that, especially now that it had been reinforced by further orders. Moreover, there was every reason to believe that the latent Christmas fellowship of the previous year had been largely displaced by an attitude hardened by the enemy's introduction of poison gas and flame throwers, the sinking of the Lusitania, and the loss of friends and comrades. In the words of 2nd-Lieutenant Llewelyn Wyn Griffith of the 15/Royal Welsh Fusiliers (113th Bde., 38th Div.), a battalion that had been in France but a few days and, under the tutelage of the 1st Guards Brigade, was in its own sector of the front line for the first time:

"We were to remain throughout possessed by the spirit of hate, answering any advances with lead. This was the substance of the message read out to us on parade on Christmas Eve."

Two companies of the battalion occupied the front line near Fauquissart and awaited Christmas Day listening to the enemy exchanging seasonal greetings with the battalion on the right of the Welsh:

"'Merry Christmas, Tommy' and 'Merry Christmas, Fritz.' As soon as it became light, we saw hands and bottles being waved at us, with encouraging shouts that we could neither understand nor misunderstand. A drunken German stumbled over his parapet and advanced through the barbed wire, followed by several others, and in a few moments there was a rush of men from both sides, carrying tins of meat, biscuits and other odd commodities for barter. This was the first time I had seen No Man's Land, and now it was Every Mans's Land, or nearly so. Some of our men would not go, and they gave terse and bitter reasons for their refusal. The officers called our men back to the line, and in a few minutes No Man's Land was once again empty and desolate. There had been a feverish exchange of 'souvenirs,' a suggestion for peace all day, and a football match in the afternoon, and a promise of no rifle fire at night. All this came to naught. An irate Brigadier came spluttering up to the line, thundering hard, throwing a 'court-martial' into every other sentence, ordering an extra dose of militant action that night, and breathing fury everywhere. We had evidently jeopardised the safety of the Allied cause."

An equally brief truce occurred not far away on the front of the 2/Scots Guards, as witnessed by Captain Wilfrid Ewart:

"A British sergeant [Sgt. J.A.L. Oliver] is shot dead almost at the outset, as he stands on the parapet. But this makes no difference. It must be an accident. The supreme craving of humanity, the irresistible, spontaneous impulse born of a common faith and a common fear, fully triumph. And so the grey and khaki figures surge towards each other as one man."

For ten minutes they met, exchanged gifts of cigars for coffee and sausages for cigarettes before parting and hastening back to their own lines as the German artillery opened fire. As a consequence of this breach of the "no fraternisation" order two officers of the Scots Guards were subsequently courtmartialled. Captain Miles Barnes was acquitted and Captain Sir Iain Colquhoun was sentenced to be reprimanded, but this was later remitted.

* * *

The reverses suffered by the British in Mesopotamia in 1915 started with the Turkish victory at the Battle of Ctesiphon in November, continued with the withdrawal of General Townsend and his force of Indian and British troops and culminated in their being besieged in Kut, "the most vile and insanitary of all the places occupied by the British in Mesopotamia."

The siege was just over two weeks old when the Turks made Christmas Eve the occasion for a determined attack that was finally beaten off, leaving their casualties scattered in the outer barbed wire defences, the wounded calling out in their helplessness throughout Christmas Day. The defenders, who had lost 315 killed, made attempts to bring in the closest Turkish wounded, but the enemy snipers prevented any attempts at providing succour until darkness fell, when a few of the casualties were brought within the perimeter. On 29th December the Turks asked for a truce to bury their dead and this was granted, but only for a period of a few hours.

Although rations for the besieged garrison were still comparatively plentiful that Christmas those manning the perimeter defences on Christmas Day had to postpone any "feast" until they were relieved and in the meantime sudden death was a constant companion. These are the observations of Captain T.E. Osmond, Medical Officer of the 2/Norfolk (18th Ind. Bde., 6th Ind. Div.):

"Sat. 25 Dec 1915: Xmas day in Fort - heavy sniping all day. Russel [Lieutenant A.R. Russel] killed. No shelling. Miserable day. Ham for Bft. & lunch...
Sun. 26 Dec 1915: ... Relieved by 76th [Punjabis]. V. quiet till noon. Had Xmas dinner midday: fish cakes - muffin - plum p. - beer & port... Church 6pm."

Godfrey Elton (later Lord Elton) of the 4/Hampshire (30th Ind. Bde., 6th Ind. Div.) recalled:

"...we were to have a Christmas breakfast - of sausages - in front line. But soon after a dust-storm got up. In a few minutes every face was a grey mask. We crouched under our blankets, but each mouthful, when the sausages came, was coated with this dust on its way to our mouths."

Kut held out until 29th April 1916 when the garrison of 13,300 British and Indian officers and men surrendered into the hands of a callous enemy whose hideous cruelty and negligence towards their captives resulted in the death of 26 per cent of the Indian rank and file prisoners, and 70 per cent of the British rank and file prisoners never returned for a Christmas at home.

1916

For the British on the Western Front 1916 was the year of The Big Push, the offensive on the Somme that lasted from the catastrophic 1st July, when the British Army lost nearly 58,000 men (of whom 19,000 were killed), to its close 419,654 casualties later on 18th November with the final attack of the Battle of the Ancre, perhaps the least understood of all the battles that made up the Somme offensive.

In the British Official History that final attack is described as: "delivered in whirling sleet which afterwards changed to rain. More abominable conditions for active warfare are hardly to be imagined: the infantry, dark figures only visible for a short distance against the white ground groped their way forward as best they could through half-frozen mud that was soon to dissolve into chalky slime." From this date on the constant rain reduced the shell blasted soil of the battlefield to a glutinous mud that another Official Historian, Cyril Falls, characterised in this way:

"Mud, for the men in the line, was no mere inorganic nuisance and obstacle. It took on an aggresive wolf-like guise, and like a wolf could pull down and swallow the lonely wanderer in the darkness. When it was at its worst no more was feasible than to hold the line and to ensure that the troops in it were fed and regularly relieved."

Life in such conditions was virtually intolerable. For example, the author's Grandfather was part of the garrison holding a waterlogged captured German trench, standing for hours at a time with muddy water well over his knees. Slowly, the feeling of intense cold left his legs and was replaced by a warm glow. When ordered to move by his sergeant he found he could not. His legs had filled with fluid, swelling them to nearly twice their natural size. There were no stretcher bearers (even assuming that they could have negotiated the mud), so his comrades hoisted him over the parados and, given rough directions, he crawled away to the regimental aid post, through the mud and over the bodies of friends and enemies. At the aid post they had to slit the legs of his trousers with a scalpel and then make incisions in his legs to drain off the putrid fluid that filled them. Eventually stretchered away from the front he was evacuated from France, spent Christmas 1916 in hospital in England and was left unfit for further service overseas.

Even these appalling conditions and the approach of a third wartime Christmas do not appear to have given rise to any overwhelming sense of disillusionment in the BEF. Instead, there seems to have been a feeling of stubborn resignation and a determination to "see it through," no matter how long the war lasted. Harry Pryce-Jones, now a Lieut.-Colonel and serving on the Staff of the 38th (Welsh) Division, wrote to his wife on 2nd December 1916:

"Another month has started and one feels we are a month nearer peace and happiness - but only by the calendar!... there appears to be no ending to this war!!"

In Pryce-Jones's old battalion, 2/Coldstream, who were holding trenches recently taken over from the French at Sailly-Saillisel, No. 2 Company was commanded by Captian William Baynes, who had joined the battalion as a 38-year old 2nd-Lieutenant in February 1915. Captain Baynes (later Sir William Baynes, Bt., and known in the battalion as "Judge" because of his pre-war appointment in the Egyptian Native Courts) was intent on ensuring that his men should have the best Christmas possible in the hideous circumstances. On 22nd December he wrote to his father:

"The Coldstream comforts have just arrived for the men, but they are such a rotten show, small tins of sweets, tubes of tooth-paste, and writing pads too small to be of any use, that I am wondering whether you would like to step into the breach and give each man in the company a respectable present."

He suggested that these gifts should comprise "60 pairs of slippers, canvas or otherwise, but soles must be strong, I think leather, sizes from 9 to 11; 60 good razors; 30 strong hand knitted prs. of socks, good size as they shrink so much." Appreciating that the slippers might be difficult to find he suggested that "about 20 of them might be replaced by woollen Balaclava helmets; these are very comforting to the men, only they are not allowed to wear them in the trenches as they cover their ears too much, and they are difficult enough to wake up without that."

The battalion spent Christmas Day in the line ("we ate Aunt Agnes' most suitable plum pudding underground") and, as was so often the case with front line units, had "to wait a few days for our more riotous

Xmas Dinner" and even this was disrupted when they were suddenly warned of an early return to the line. Baynes wrote to his mother on 7th January 1917 from billets at Meaulte:

"The whole battalion had their Xmas dinners yesterday in a great hurry and for fear that they would never get them at all, all our agreeable little plans having been knocked on the head. The dinners were rather a scramble, as we have not yet reached civilisation, and we were unable to get plates or glasses for the men; however No 2 managed to raise a piano, and after eating 1 lb pork, ½ 1b cauliflowers, ½ 1b plum pudding, [and] 2¼ pints of beer per man, followed by bread and butter and cheese, and rum and hot water, they kept up a cheerful concert till about 8 o'c (the dinner started at 1), and there is no one in the guard room this morning. They ate your plum puddings, which were greatly appreciated, and there was enough for anyone who could manage it to have a second helping. The sergeants are having their dinner tomorrow, if we are still here.

Father's kind presents are just beginning to arrive, and will, I think, be a great success; the shoes [slippers] are excellent, and the Sgt. Major tells me everyone will want them, but I am afraid they will not get below the rank of N.C.O. They all seem to like the razors, as the ration issue are so bad and very difficult to shave with."

Festive meals of the proportions enjoyed by the Coldstream were by no means unusual, but for new arrivals who had yet to join their unit there was no Yuletide greeting, no traditional meal and no cheerful concert. Private Digby Stone of the Honourable Artillery Company was part of a draft that had embarked for France on Christmas Eve:

"Xmas day about 7am found us in the harbour at Havre. We were none too merry after a most wretched night. After disembarking we marched to Harfleur Camp 5 miles away along a wretched road. Dinner consisted of ½ pint of cold stew which was soon finished and we then set to work fixing up bell tents, 17 men in each tent were crowded for the night... Rain fell heavily during the night and as the tent I was in was old we all got well soaked by the morning."

Prior to his embarkation at Southampton Private Stone had been "put to work loading up boats with Xmas parcels... piled up on the quay like sacks of corn." Some 4¾ million parcels were sent to France in the four weeks prior to Christmas 1916, but there are no surviving figures for the homeward bound flow of parcels and cards.

The sheer quantity of Christmas post and the weather conditions brought the APS near to breaking point. Oliver Lyttelton (later Viscount Chandos) was serving with the 3/Grenadier (2nd Gds, Bde., Gds., Div.):

"The mails are ghastly; it takes about ten days for letters to get out so all one's supplies are disorganised. It doesn't matter so much that the letters are old as long as they come more or less regularly, but it is annoying when butter is stale and so on."

The recommended gifts this year included numerous items of stationery (Lady Baynes sent her son specially printed writing-paper) and a particular favourite was the "'Swan' active service writing kit." This comprised a Swan fountain pen, a special metal pen holder that clipped inside a breast pocket and a supply of soluble ink tablets and cost 14s 4d (72p): "And what a capital Christmas present!"

With the growth of the BEF far more cards were being designed and printed for the troops, and their production was now a staff problem, not to say a headache.

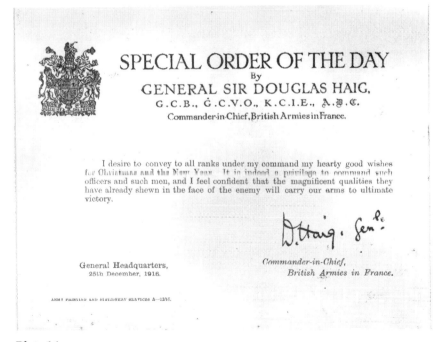

Plate 14

On 2nd December 1916 Lieut.-Colonel S.G. Partridge, Director of the Army Printing and Stationery Services was "warned" by the General Staff "that a sketch of Sir Douglas Haig is to be distributed to the troops for Christmas." He was instructed to print two million copies. No reason was given when the order was cancelled only three days later. Haig simply issued a Special Order of the Day to convey "to all ranks under my command my hearty good wishes for Christmas and the New Year" (see *Plate 14*). Haig's principal Christmas gift was promotion to Field-Marshal fróm 1st January 1917.

In the 38th Division the producion of Christmas Cards was made the responsibility of the Adjutant and Quartermaster General's Branch, and specifically the Assistant Adjutant-General, Harry Pryce-Jones. He ordered 25,000 copies of a design that incorporated a rather handsome dragon (the divisional sign) over seasonal greetings in Welsh with the text of "Land of My Fathers" inside (see *Colour Plate 2*). There were two versions, one with the dragon in red and the other with the dragon in gilt and a red and green ribbon tie. By 13th November sufficient orders had been received for Pryce-Jones to say they were selling "like hot cakes," but by 16th December only a few had actually been delivered by the (unknown) printers. On 23rd December he complained that "20,000 Red Dragon cards are still absent," though on the 24th he had heard of them "being on their way from Havre." They didn't turn up on Christmas Day, but the divisional headquarters was in too festive a mood to worry too much, as recorded in the A and Q Staff War Diary:

"The men attached to Headquarters... had their Christmas Dinner at 1pm in the Garage Esquelbecq. About 250 sat down to a dinner consisting of Turkey, Goose, Pork, Vegetables and Christmas Pudding. The health of the King was proposed by the Camp Commandant, to which the men heartily responded."

In fact the cards didn't turn up until after Boxing Day, but happily Pryce-Jones's fear that the divisional comforts fund "may lose £120... if the men won't buy them" was not justified.

The staff of the 14th (Light) division encountered different problems when their card attracted the attention of the BEF's censor. Its design showed the "N E Corner of Delville Wood" (captured by the division on 27th August) with the relevant map reference. The card was withdrawn and the printers, Raphael Tuck & Sons, overprinted the offending line

with an obscuring design (see *Colour Plate 3*).

It was virtually impossible to celebrate the religious festival of Christmas in the line, but Captain F.C. Hitchcock's company of 2/Leinsters (73rd Bde., 24th Div.) came very close in the support line near Loos:

"The men built a small altar in a large fire bay, with sand-bags, and all attended with the exception of the gas sentries. All the Company officers... were present, with the exception of Sharp, who had been attached to B Company in the front line. The service lasted some 25 minutes. It was undoubtedly the most impressive I have ever attended.

We were about 120 strong, crowded into some large fire bays... holding our steel helmets and listening with bowed heads to the Padre. The whole area was covered in snow, and lay thick on the parapets and parados. An occasional enemy shell whined overhead, to explode in the Loos shambles. The whole atmosphere seemed in keeping with a Christmas Day in the trenches."

Meanwhile, at the close of the year in Mesopotamia, Captain L.W. Jardine of the 5/Royal West Surrey (12th Ind. Bde., 15th Ind. Div.) was reviewing his service life in a letter to his father:

"This should reach you about Christmas which will be the third consecutive Christmas that I have been away. A lot of fellows talk about wasting the best years of our lives at this game but I don't agree. We are getting the adventures and experiences which I at any rate always hoped to have before I settled down to my life's job...".

1917

As 1917 drew to its close the British army could look back on yet another year of brutal endeavour for very little obvious gain.

On the Western Front the BEF's year had been dominated by the Third Battle of Ypres, commonly known as Passchendaele, that had lasted from the final day of July until mid-November. Its wearing down effect had been more or less equal on both sides and only in saving the mutinous French army from probing German attacks did it have any immediate beneficial effect.

There had been some small successes: the capture of Vimy Ridge at the outset of the Battle of Arras in April, the Battle of Messines in June where another ridge had been captured by having its heart blown out by 19 deep mines, and briefly, the Battle of Cambrai in November. However, this, the first mass tank attack, had outrun its own strength in ten days and a German counter-attack took back as much ground as had been gained.

Moreover, the entry of the Americans into the war in April (four divisions totalling 130,000 men were in France by 1st December) and the imminent collapse of the Eastern Front, releasing many German divisions for the Western Front, were harbingers of a war of a very different character in 1918.

At last, in early December, came the good news from Palestine of the capture of Jerusalem. But even there foul winter weather was not unknown. Private S.F. Hatton was with the 1st County of London (Middlesex) Yeomanry encamped at Askelon:

"In many respects it was a most wretched Christmas; a torrential downpour began two days before, and lasted well over a week. We were not in tents, our only cover being single sheets, and thus by the time the 'Happy Morn' arrived, our blankets, kit, and the clothes we stood up in were saturated. A couple of native sheep had been bought for the feast, but it rained so heavily, that it was impossible to get a fire going to roast them, so that dinner had to be postponed till the evening, and even then all Charlie's resource could produce nothing better than an under cooked watery stew.

...The main trouble, however, was that the rain was so terrific that it was impossible for the men to foregather anywhere, and thus we had to celebrate, by two and threes, cramped in dripping 'bivies' and much of the joyousness of the Festival was lost. It certainly was strange spending Christmas so near to Bethlehem, where had been born the Babe whose advent founded Christendom."

Late December 1917 on the Western Front was marked by an exceedingly bitter frost, followed by a seasonal fall of snow. Lieutenant Huntly Gordon in an artillery forward observation post near Bapaume described:

"28 degrees of frost, a record even for this savagely cold winter. We have no means of keeping warm, as there is barely room to swing our arms. To avoid being seen we have to be in position before daylight, and only leave at dusk. By that time we are nearly dead with cold. My feet were sore to begin with, but we were fairly staggering on the way home. We have this joy-trip every fourth day. Thank God, it won't be my turn on Christmas Day."

Another artillery officer, on the other side of the wire, Leutnant Herbert Sulzbach, was writing at the same time: "Our fourth Christmas is nearly upon us, and thank God, the front-line spirit still stands supreme above any feelings of doubt." Sulzbach also commented on the weather: "...all this snow is quite unusual for France. Whether you look at it from the guns, or from the sentry posts, the landscape looks more and more innocent."

And in such weather innocence could be found even in the dour surroundings of the British GHQ at Montreuil where Lieut.-Colonel Harry Pryce-Jones had been appointed Assistant Adjutant-General on 5th December:

"It is snowing again and as the ground is already deep in snow, it doesn't add to one's comfort. As we all walk from here to the club for luncheon, some children, more particularly a girl about 10 years old, always snowball us and enjoy it fearfully!" And on the following day: "Still bitterly cold and I feel that the snow will remain on the ground for weeks. That little girl does so enjoy snowballing all the officers as they go to luncheon past her cottage.

However, one officer rolled her in the snow yesterday, which added to her pleasure and didn't damp her ardour one bit."

Even the Adjutant-General's staff at GHQ enjoyed a little innocent fun on Christmas Day:

"We really had quite a cheerful dinner - had crackers, wore caps and played at children! Got in a piano, danced and did silly things till 11.30; personally I only looked on, but I must admit I laughed a good deal."

The freezing weather had at least one advantage, as noted by the newly arrived Private Douglas Wills of the 78th Battalion, Canadian Expeditionary Force, in a letter to his parents in Winnipeg: "The ground is frozen and snow covered, so there is no mud as yet for which we are thankful".

Like many other Imperial troops Wills had relatives in Britain who kept him supplied with comforts:

"In the last two days four parcels have been brought up for me by the ration parties. They are all from the aunts and uncles in England so am having plenty of good things for Xmas...Well, it isn't everyone who has spent Xmas up here, so it is something to look back on and is about the most novel Christmas a man could spend. I guess Fritzie will send us some Xmas boxes of hate as he has been the last few days. We have been lucky in the way of rations - bacon and butter and bread even up here and raspberry and apricot jam."

Wills spent his Christmas day in the front line: "Fine day, on duty in trench 4-6pm. Pudding, cake, tin of cherries, bread, butter, marmalade, damson jam. Heavy snow at night."

For units lucky enough to be out of the line there was the chance to attend Christmas Day services under cover from the elements. The 8/Royal Berkshire (1st Bde., 1st Div.) were billeted in Farms and shelters at Reninghof when Private Frank Gray's platoon attended such a service at a Church Army Hut:

It was a service simple but impressive. The Christmas hymns seemed to be roared rather than sung, so great was the volume of sound from rough male voices. I had never heard the officiating Chaplain before. For that packed audience of war-worn men it was a great sermon. He besought us with much earnestness on this birthday of the Prince of Peace to pray devoutly that peace might come again to the world, and we were all greatly impressed when, sobbing like a child, he concluded his sermon with the words: 'Boys, notwith-standing all the mud and blood, there is a God!...' He must have known by the proportion of the congregation who remained for the Communion service that his appeal had not fallen on deaf ears."

At the 38th Division the order for their 1917 card (see *Plate 15*) was increased from the 25,000 of 1916 to 45,000. Moreover, this year they were delivered in good time and the entire stock was sold out by 16th December! Part of the proceeds went toward providing a special Christmas dinner on 30th December for "the girls employed at the Divisional laundry."

The profits of £248 10s 6d from the sale of the first Labour Corps card (see *Plate 16*) were handed to the Central Prisoners of War Committee for the benefit of Labour Corps prisoners.

Christmas Day was not marked by any alleviation in the privations and sufferings of some prisoners of war. These two accounts are by prisoners who in peacetime had been on the staff of the Prudential Assurance Company, a firm that attempted to send parcels to their employee prisoners:

"It was particularly cold on Christmas Day, which made the absence of fuel still more noticeable. A very gloomy day and darkness fell at about three o'clock.

Our rations did not arrive until six in the evening and consisted of stinking fish-roe, so salt that we could scarcely swallow it, and rotten potatoes boiled in their jackets." (W.S. Casserley).

Plate 15

· Labor · omnia · vincit ·

BELIEVE IN YOUR MISSION, GREET LIFE
WITH A CHEER; THERE'S A BIG WORK
TO DO, AND THAT'S WHY YOU ARE HERE.
R. W. Service

Plate 16

"Mr. W. Allan was in Cologne on Christmas Day, 1917. For him, also, this was a day far removed from festivity. He and some forty odd prisoners were earmarked for a parade through the streets of the city, while the people crowded the footpaths to jeer and laugh as they passed along. At noon the prisoners were marched to a military barracks for a plate of cabbage soup and a piece of black bread, their first food for over twenty-four hours."

Major W.A.A Phillips of the 24th Punjabis was one of the officers captured at the fall of Kut and spent his Christmas in a prison camp at Changra in Turkey. Writing home on 6th January 1918 he complained:

"It is now over 6 weeks since any of us had any letters whatever. Of course we have had a lot of frost and snow, but it is not bad enough to stop our letters coming through. It's very sickening, especially at Xmas time, but what can one expect?

We had rather a sad time at Xmas. We were allowed to go out tobogganing on the afternoon of Xmas day and had some quite good fun, in spite of a rough course and numerous falls, but as we were coming back to Barracks afterwards a B[ritish]. O[fficer]., Major Corbett [Major R.D. de la C. Corbett, 48th Pioneers, attached RFC], was suddenly taken ill and died almost immediately on getting to his room. The doctors were not able to determine what was the matter but seem to think it may have been a case of mountain sickness... He was buried next day, the coffin being drawn on one of the toboggans."

On 3rd December Haig had informed his Army Commanders that "the general situation on the Russian and Italian fronts, combined with the paucity of reinforcements which we are likely to receive, will in all probability necessitate our adopting a defensive attitude for the next few months. We must be prepared to meet a strong and sustained hostile offensive."

Br.-General John Charteris, Haig's departing intelligence chief, told the Commander-in-Chief on 20th December that the enemy's offensive would fall in March and on Christmas Day recorded:

"The fourth Christmas at war, and though the outlook is so black, yet still I think it will be the last War Christmas. ... We cannot fail to win. Each year inevitably shows success more certain, but for the next few months the prospect is the most gloomy since 1914".

FOUR YEARS AGO!

Plate 17

1918

For the next three months the BEF held its breath waiting for the blow to fall. When it came, on 21st March, it was harder, went deeper and was then repeated more often than even Charteris had expected. But this time it was the Germans who outran their strength. A balance of forces was achieved for a brief period and then, from 18th July 1918, the advantage of weight and strength lay with the Allies. Led by the British they inflicted a series of defeats on the German army, including its "black day" on 8th August, that led to an armistice on 11th November. Elsewhere, Bulgaria had sued for peace, Turkey had capitulated and the Austro-Hungarian Empire had crumbled.

In Britain news of the Armistice led to the release of pent up emotions that fuelled wild celebrations that were in great contrast to the restraint with which the news was generally received by the fighting units of the BEF. Lieut.-Colonel B.H. Puckle of the 57th Battalion, Machine Gun Corps (57th Div.), described the reactions of many when he wrote on 12th November:

> "Things have been very quiet here, and I've seen no signs of rejoicing or revelry by night... People took it so quietly. I think perhaps it is because we have not collected our ideas yet, and haven't quite realised what has happened to us."

When they did realise what had happened to them the requirements for the vast majority were simple: leave or demobilisation, preferably the latter. A few men were demobilised, mostly miners, whose services were urgently required at home, and for some others there was Christmas leave, but the majority spent Christmas with their units in France or the British occupied area of the Rhineland.

This year their cards not only reflected pride in past achievements, particularly the victories of the "Last 100 Days," but also looked forward to a return to civilian life, sometimes compared with the joys of pre-war days. An example is that of the 24th Division (see *Plate 17*).

For those, including many returned prisoners of war, who were in London on Christmas Day 1918, there was a hearty welcome (the War Chest Club provided a "great iced cake weighing 2½ cwt.") and the weather was bright and crisp, with a touch of frost, as great crowds strolled about, wishing one another the compliments of the season.

Captain F.C. Hitchcock didn't quite make it home in time and on Christmas Day was aboard a cross-channel steamer:

"I was detailed to inspect the men in their life-belts, which they donned with much 'grousing.' Though the submarine menace was over, yet there was always the chance of bumping into a drifting mine. I came across a man who had belonged to my platoon at Ypres 1n 1915 - Pte. Eldridge - now a Sapper; much water and blood had flowed under the bridge since those far away days in 'Fifteen,' and together we wondered how many men of the old platoon could answer the roll call this Christmas Day.

As we talked the giant cliffs of Dover loomed out in their whiteness against the evening sky."

Plate 19: 1914 - Private card - Obverse: A patriotic "private" card (one where the name and address of the sender were printed inside) for 1914. This example was sent by a Private Frank Saxby stationed at Closterdale Camp, North Yorkshire.

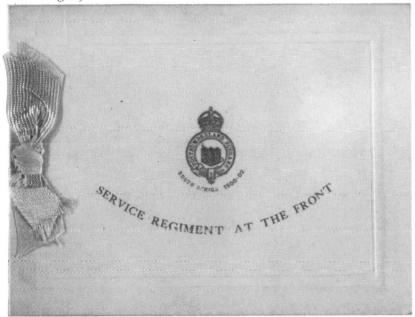

Plate 18: 1914 - 1/Northumberland Hussars - Obverse: The 1/Northumberland (Hussars) Yeomanry provided the mounted troops for the 7th Division when it was formed between August and October, 1914. The regiment landed at Zeebrugge on 6th October 1914 and served with the division until broken up as divisional cavalry in April 1915. It was re-formed in May 1916 and served with various corps until the end of the war.

With Best Wishes for Christmas
and the New Year.

From .

Sergt. John. A. Arnold.
No 2028

Plates 20 & 21: 1915 - Motor MG Service - Obverse and Inside: The Motor Machine Gun Service was formed late in 1914 and initially drew its personnel from the Royal Field Artillery. Equipped with motorcycle combinations that mounted .303-inch Vickers machine guns, the MMGS was intended to provide a highly mobile force that could bring concentrated fire power to bear in attack or defence. It was absorbed by the Machine Gun Corps when that corps was formed in November 1915 and many of its officers and men later transferred to the Tank Corps when several of the motor batteries were disbanded. However, the few surviving batteries acquitted themselves well during the 1918 March Retreat and the Advance to Victory. The illustration inside this 1915 card appears to be of a Royal Enfield combination where the Vickers was mounted facing to the rear. Firing whilst on the move, as shown here, must have been an exceedingly uncertain business.

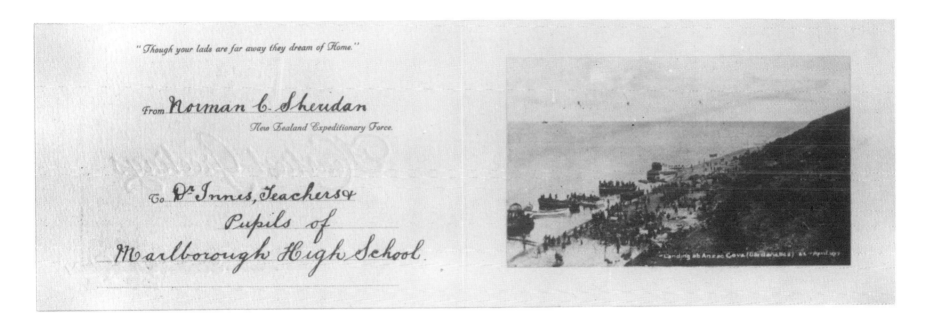

"*Though your lads are far away they dream of Home.*"

From Norman C. Sheridan

New Zealand Expeditionary Force.

To Dr Innes, Teachers &
Pupils of
Marlborough High School

Plate 22: 1915 - Anzac Cove - Inside: The evacuation of Anzac Cove was completed on 20th December 1915, just about the time that this card would have reached Marlborough on the South Island of New Zealand.

Plates 23 & 24: 1915 - 1/6 Hampshire - Obverse and Inside: The 1/6 (Duke of Connaught's Own) Battalion, Hampshire Regiment, was one of seven Hampshire Territorial Force battalions that served in India during the war. They arrived in November 1914 and remained until September 1917 when they joined the 52nd Indian Brigade in Mesopotamia. There were serious concerns behind the humorous doggerel verse. The first Zeppelin raid on Britain had been carried out by three German naval airships on the night of the 19/20th January 1915 and between April and October there were a further nineteen raids. The heaviest, by five Zeppelins on the night of 13/14th October, had resulted in 71 killed and 128 injured.

Although from "Zeps" out here we're free
We think of you across the Sea
And would endure them could we be
With you
this
Xmas.

From

Pte J. H. Barnes

Agra India
1915.

1/6th (D.C.O.) Bn Hampshire Regt.

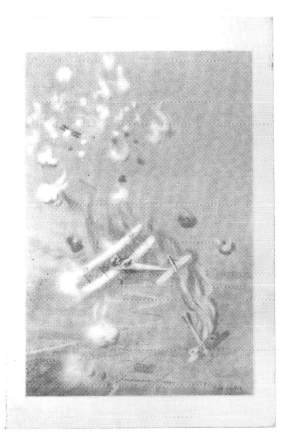

Plates 25 & 26: 1915 - RFC - Obverse and Inside: The Royal Flying Corps called on one of their own pilots to provide the illustration for their 1915 card. Lt.-Col. Harold Wyllie, OBE (1880-1973) produced this delicate sketch of a violent dogfight, showing what appears to be a BE2c shooting down a German aircraft, while "archie" bursts all around. Wyllie, better known as a marine artist, is represented in the collection of the Imperial War Museum by a number of oil paintings depicting the air war over the Western Front.

Plate 28: 1916 - 61st Division - Obverse: The 61st (2/South Midland) Division was a second line (or reserve) Territorial Force division that had arrived in France in late May 1916.

Plate 27: 1915 - Doberitz - Obverse: Doberitz, near Potsdam, was the site of a large Prisoner-of-War camp. This particular example of their 1915 card, designed by Cecil A. Tooke of the Royal Naval Division, was sent by prisoner Alick Knowles, RNR to a Miss Grace Davis in Leith.

DEFENDERS OF THE EMPIRE.

Colour Plate 1 [see Page 5]

Colour Plate 2 [see Page 16]

Colour Plate 3 [see Page 16]

Colour Plate 4: 1917 - 4th Div. - Obverse: The 4th Division's 1917 card was designed by 2/Lt. A.E. Coles of the 1/Somerset Light Infantry (11th Brigade).

Colour Plate 5: 1917 - Corps Topo. Section - Obverse: A Topographical Section was formed for each corps on the Western Front during the autumn of 1916. Each section had an establishment of one officer, five draughtsmen, and three topographers. Its transport comprised two motorcycles, "one having a sidecar." Apart from work on fixing the location of enemy artillery for counter battery work, the section's primary duty during operations was to produce maps giving the latest information as early as possible each morning. Since section printing equipment was limited to an Ellam duplicator, it seems reasonable to assume that the cards were printed at a Field Survey Company.

Colour Plate 6: 1917 - 11th Div. - Obverse: The 11th (Northern) Division was a New Army formation that had served in Gallipoli and Egypt before arriving in France in July 1916. In 1917 it had been heavily engaged in the Third Battle of Ypres and in 1918 it would see equally heavy fighting in the Advance to Victory.

Colour Plate 7: 1917 - 56th Div. - Obverse: A. Wakefield of the Queen's Westminster Rifles (16/London) was apparently serving with the headquarters of the 56th (London) Division, TF, when he designed this remarkably intricate 1917 card that was yet another Raphael Tuck & Sons production. as can be seen, the divisional sign was the short sword ("Wat Tyler's dagger"), from the arms of the City of London. The same artist also designed a similar, though much smaller, card for the division for Christmas 1918.

Colour Plate 8: 1917 - 63rd Div. - Inside: Another production by Devambez of Paris, this time for the 63rd (Royal Naval) Division, hence the reference to the "salt" on the tail of the German prisoner. At Christmas 1917 the RND was holding the line on Welsh Ridge, near Marcoing on the Cambrai front. The Germans launched an assault here on 30th December and during the fighting Lieut.-Commander Patrick Shaw-Stewart, temporarily commanding Hood Battalion, was killed in action. "Of that small band of scholars, poets and men of letters who had served in the Naval Division in Gallipoli, he had been almost the last survivor." (Divisional history.)

Colour Plate 9: 1917 - Salonika - Obverse: This 1917 Christmas greeting from Salonika was designed by Lieut.-Colonel George Denholm Armour, OBE (1864-1949), a well-known painter of equestrian portraits and illustrator of Surtees and other works of hunting, shooting and fishing literature. During his service in Salonika he commanded first No. 42 Remount Squadron and then the Remount Depot. The card was printed by No. 8 Survey Company, RE.

Colour Plate 10: 1917 - IX Corps - Obverse: The unknown artist of this 1917 card for IX Corps cleverly incorporated the Corps sign, a bow and arrow, elements of the crest of Lieut.-General Sir Alexander Hamilton-Gordon, the Corps' first commander in France. The design also incorporates a reference to the part played by the Corps in the successful Second Army assault on the Messines Ridge on 7th June 1917.

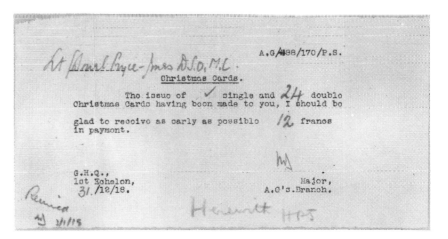

Colour Plate 11: 1917 - 39th Div. - Inside: The Pioneer Brealey who provided the illustration for the inside of the 39th Division's 1917 card was William Ramsden Brealey, ROI, RBA (1889-1949), a portrait painter, who probably served with 13/Gloucester, the division's pioneer battalion. It is possible that his subject for this portrait was a fellow pioneer. The Obverse of this card appears on the back of the jacket.

Colour Plate 12: 1917 - 14th Div. - Inside: This 1917 card for the 14th (Light) Division was yet another production by Raphael Tuck & Sons. The artist of the study of men and mules transporting ammunition across the winter battlefield is unknown.

Colour Plate 13: 1918 - GHQ - Obverse: The GHQ card for 1918 shows the gateway to the courtyard of their main offices in the Ecole Militaire, Montreuil. The cards were printed by the Army Printing and Stationary Services and in the version shown here were sold at 50 centimes each (*vide* request for payment for 24 cards bought by Lt.-Col. Harry Pryce-Jones; illustrated on previous page.)

Colour Plate 14: 1918 - IWT - Obverse: It is wholly forgotten today, but by the time of the Armistice the Inland Water Transport service of the BEF was a huge organisation. It had a strength of 10,680 officers and men who operated nearly 1,000 tugs, barges and other craft, carrying 38,000 tons of stores per week on the rivers and canals of France. Moreover, there was a coastwise convoy system and a cross-Channel barge service under their control that had a fleet of over 380 vessels.

Plates 29 & 30: 1916 - 12th Division - Obverse and Inside: After having been heavily engaged in the Battle of the Somme the 12th (Eastern) Division was fortunate enough to spend Christmas 1916 out of the line. As its title implies it was formed largely from Kitchener Army units raised in East Anglia and the eastern home counties, but its "Ace of Spades" divisional sign had no particular significance. Their history describes how a "ton of divisional cards arrived for dispatch to our friends" so, even allowing for some exageration, it is surprising just how scarce this card appears to be. The striking drawing (by an unknown artist) of German prisoners being escorted down a communication trench during a night attack does not appear to relate to any specfic divisional operation.

Plates 31 & 32: 1916 - 8th Division - Obverse and Inside: The artist of this ingenious cut out 1916 card for the 8th Division is thought to be Lieutenant C. Ambler, 1/Sherwood Foresters. He served in France from October 1914 to November 1917, and from April 1918 to June 1918, was wounded and mentioned in despatches.

Plate 34: 1916 - 80 Field Coy. RE - Obverse: After heavy fighting throughout the Somme campaign the 18th Division, including the 80th Field Company, RE, was withdrawn to the Abbeville area for a well-earned Christmas rest that lasted until mid-January 1917.

Plate 33: 1916 - 119 Coy. RE - Obverse: Contrary to the impression given by the illustration on their 1916 card the 119th Company, RE, was not a tunnelling company, but a Railway Construction Company. They had arrived in France the previous May to join the other railway companies in laying and maintaining broad guage track in preparation for the Battle of the Somme. By December 1916 there were 22 railway construction companies in France and during the year they had put down 417 miles of track.

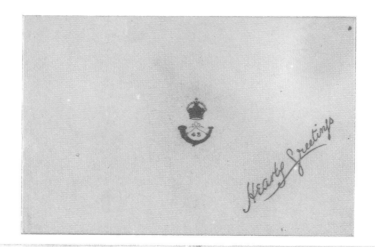

OUR CAMP, MESOPOTAMIA, NOVEMBER 1916.

Plates 35 & 36: 1916 - 1/Ox. & Bucks - Obverse and Inside: At the outbreak of war the 1/Oxford and Buckinghamshire Light Infantry (the old 43rd Regiment) had been stationed in India and in November 1914 had moved with the 6th (Poona) Division to Mesopotamia. Its survivors were taken prisoner on the surrender of Kut on 29th April 1916. A new battalion was created in July 1916 and after service on the Lines of Communication it joined the 15th Division in October 1917. It remained in Mesopotamia for the rest of the war.

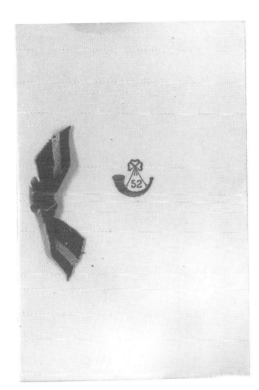

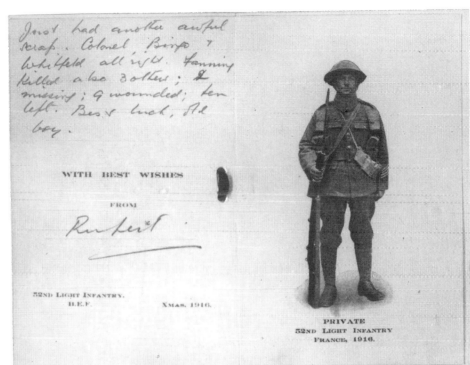

Just had another awful scrap. Colonel Bingo ? Whitfield all right. Fanning killed ... two Brothers; & missing; 9 wounded; ten left. Best of luck, old boy.

WITH BEST WISHES

FROM

Rupert

52ND LIGHT INFANTRY. B.E.F.   XMAS. 1916.

PRIVATE
52ND LIGHT INFANTRY
FRANCE, 1916.

Plates 37 & 38: 1916 - 2/Ox. & Bucks - Obverse and Inside: The 2/Oxford and Buckinghamshire Light Infantry (the old 52nd Regiment) had landed in France in August 1914 as part of the 2nd Division and served with them on the Western Front throughout the war. This example was sent to an officer serving with the 1st Battalion in Mesopotamia and the sender's message must have made bitter reading. The "scrap" referred to was the battalion's part in the Battle of the Ancre (13th-16th November 1916), during which six officers were killed in action, including Captain V.E. Fanning.

THE CITADEL, CAIRO.

Plates 39 & 40: 1916 - 22/Rifle Brigade - Obverse and Inside: The 22/ (Wessex & Welsh) Rifle Brigade was one of seven Territorial battalions of the Regiment formed in November 1915 for garrison duties overseas. It was sent first to Egypt and then suddenly transferred to Salonika in November 1916, hence the photograph of Cairo but the message from Salonika in this example of their 1916 card. Garrison battalions were never intended for front line service, being made up of "elderly men, sometimes old regular soldiers, and younger men unfitted, by reason of wounds or other disabilities, for hard work or exposure." Nevertheless, five such battalions, including the 22/Rifle Brigade, were formed into the 228th Brigade (administered by the 28th Division) in Salonika and became front line units.

Plates 41 & 42: 1916 - 20th Div. - Obverse & Inside: The 20th (Light) Division was another formation that saw heavy fighting on the Somme, particularly at Guillemont, which the Division captured on 3rd September, as commemorated in the drawing by the *Punch* artist L. Raven Hill (1867-1942) inside the division's 1916 card. This was one of a number of cards printed by G. Devambez in Paris. Their productions often used designs by an artist who signed his work with a "CP" monogram and they usually reproduced a calendar for the forthcoming year on the reverse of their cards.

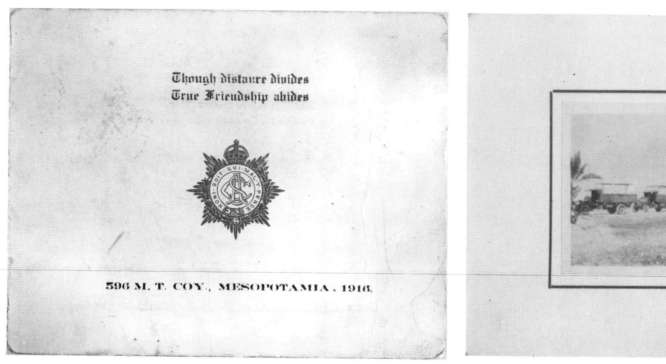

Plates 43 & 44: 1916 - 596 M.T. Coy. - Obverse and Inside: No. 596 M.T. Company, ASC, had arrived in Mesopotamia from Egypt in January 1916. It had a strength of some 400 officers and men and was equipped with 110 3-ton Peerless lorries, some of which are shown in the photograph used inside their 1916 card.

Plate 46: 1916 - 51st Div. - Obverse: That Scottish units and formations tended to set greater emphasis on the celebration of the New Year rather than Christmas is confirmed by this card designed by the Scottish etcher and engraver Leonard J. Smith (1885-?) for the 51st (Highland) Division to send greetings for the New Year of 1917.

Plate 45: 1916 - RTO - Obverse: Most stations that handled the BEF's railway traffic on the Western Front had a Railway Transport Officer and, in the terms of the official manual, his "military authority... whatever his rank may be, will, as regards the movements of troops and their accessories by rail, be paramount at the station where he is posted for duty." Such power inevitably led to RTOs becoming a much maligned group, frequently characterised as unhelpful and obstructive. But they were often wounded or sick officers, appointed RTOs while unfit for further front line service. Faced with duties that, even for fit men, were often onerous and complex, it is not surprising if some of them were soured by their tasks.

Plate 47: 1917 - ROD - Obverse: The initials of the BEF's Railway Operating
Division painted on the sides of their locomotives, as seen here in a 1917
card, were often translated by weary soldiers as meaning "Roll on Duration."
By the close of the war the ROD on the Western Front was employing 48
Railway Operating Companies to run the trains on the British broad gauge
railways and three of these companies were drawn from Australian troops.

Plates 48 & 49: 1917 - HMS Sir Thomas Picton - Obverse and Inside: HMS *Sir Thomas Picton* was a 5,900 ton *Lord Clive* Class Monitor, armed with two 12-inch guns. Built by Harland and Wolff, Belfast, this shallow draft, slow moving, armoured coastal bombardment warship was launched on 30th September 1915 and served in the Mediterranean 1915-1918. She was named for Lieut.-General Sir Thomas Picton, who died while leading his second brigade in a charge at Waterloo and for such a ponderous warship (6½ knots maximum) she had an appropriate giant tortoise as her crest and an equally appropriate motto in *Festina Lente*: Hasten Slowly. Ironically, when sold for scrap in 1921 she was towed across the North Sea and broken up in Germany.

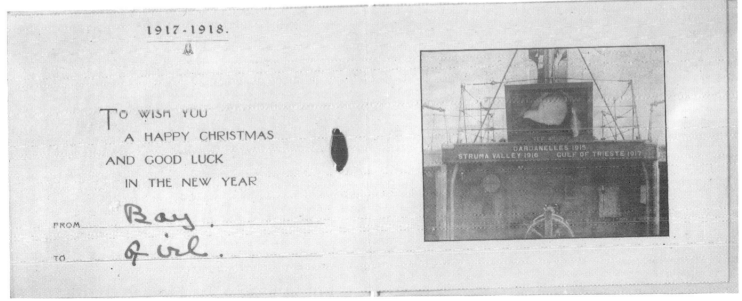

SOMME
PERONNE
YPRES

48th DIVISION

XMAS 1917

Plate 50 [facing page]: 1917 - 48th Div. - Obverse: The 1917 card of the 48th (South Midland) Division must be one of the largest and most unusual produced during the war. In the version shown here it was mounted on heavy card with punch holes in the upper margin so that it could be suspended from a ribbon. In another version it was printed on thin card and folded. The image is reproduced here full size. The design of Western Front scenes, by Driver Percy Vignale, ASC, of the 48th Divisional Train, was the winner of a divisional Christmas card competition. However, as it was being distributed the division was moving from France to Italy. Lieut.-Colonel G.H. Barnett of the division's A & G Staff considered that: "Most of the units had a very successful Christmas. They had been able to buy turkeys or pigs, and, with the aid of ration plum-puddings, canteen stores, and beer from Padova, they were able to give their men the best Christmas dinner during the war "

Plate 51: 1917 - No. 16 Squadron RFC - Obverse: At Christmas 1917 No. 16 Squadron, Royal Flying Corps, was stationed at Camblain-l'Abbe, near Aubigny, and was equipped with RE8 two-seat reconnaissance aircraft. Commanded by Major C.F.A. Portal, DSO, MC (later Marshal of the Royal Air Force Viscount Portal) the Squadron was attached to the Canadian Corps and provided them with contact patrols and artillery observation flights.

Plate 53: 1917 - Employment Base Depot - Obverse. A Lines-of-Communication Christmas card sent home to his wife by Lt.-Col. C.J.Huskinson, officer commanding No. 3 Employment Base Depot at Etaples, one of the most important training and reinforcement centres for the BEF with facilities to cater for 100,000 men.

Plate 52: 1917 - 4th Brigade RFC - Inside: 4th Brigade RFC included No. 19 Squadron, one of whose pilots, Captain (later Air Commodore) Patrick Huskinson MC, sent this card home. The squadron flew their last offensive patrol with Spads on 29th December 1917 on which occasion Captain Huskinson shot down two enemy aircraft. Soon after, the squadron was re-equipped with Sopwith Dolphins, but the machine depicted is in fact an RE8 (see *Plate 51* above). The artist identifies himself by the signature "Lenden," nothing is known about him, but his style was obviously influenced by W. Heath Robinson.

Plate 54: 1917 - 4th Dragoon Gds. - Inside: The 4th (Royal Irish) Dragoon Guards served on the Western Front with the 2nd Cavalry Brigade (1st Cavalry Division) throughout the war.

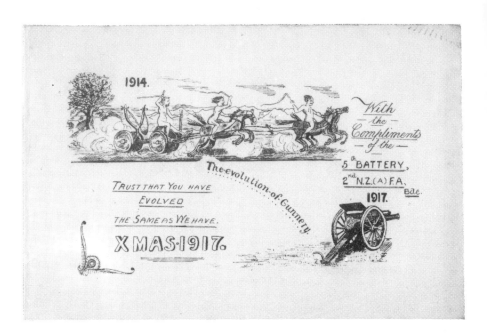

Plate 56: 1917 - 2nd NZ FA Bde. - Obverse: The 2nd New Zealand Field Artillery Brigade was detached from the New Zealand Division and served as an army troops unit with the Third army from January 1917 to the end of the war.

Plate 55: 1917 - XIII Corps Cyclists - Obverse: The XIII Corps Cyclist Battalion was formed in May 1916 from various cyclist companies, including those of the 18th and 30th Divisions. At Christmas 1917 the battalion was billeted at Acq, six miles north west of Arras, with detachments on duty with the Corps observation section. [see also *Plate 74*]

Plate 57: 1917 - ?Lancs Fus/E.Lancs R. - Inside: It is not known for certain which unit produced this card for Christmas 1917. However, the use of the red rose of Lancaster and the pictorial references to service in Egypt (1914), Gallipoli (1915), Egypt again (1916) and then France (1917) suggests a Territorial Force battalion of either the Lancashire Fusiliers or the East Lancashire Regiment.

Plate 58: 1917 - 24th Div. - Obverse: The 24th Division was a New Army formation that served in France from September 1915 until the Armistice. In that time it lost 35,362 officers and men, killed, wounded and missing.

Plate 59: 1917 - 66th Div.- Obverse and *[facing page]* Inside: The 1917 card of the 66th (East Lancashire) Division, a second line Territorial Force formation, that had arrived in France as recently as the previous March. It was to suffer heavily during the German offensive of March 1918 and as a result of its losses it was reduced to cadre until re-formed in the following September.

The Toast of the "Clickety Click"

Here's to my dear ones in Blighty.
And here's to our Allies true.
And here's to our pals in Khaki.
And here's to our boys in blue.

Although this Christmas finds us,
On Flanders muddy plain.
When we've beaten the Hun, and the War is done;
We'll come marching home again.

But while there's any fighting,
And Huns are massing thick;
You can safely bet, its "Hell" they'll get;
From the Boys of the "Clickety Click".

To   17ᵗʰ Division

From   G.O.C. 66ᵗʰ Division

The Hun (with Christmas Parcel.)
"Now for a good Blow-out"

Plates 60 & 61: 1917 *and* 1918 - 7th Div. - Obverse of both: The 7th Division was another that was moved from France to Italy shortly before Christmas 1917. This was the second year that their card was designed by John Prinsep Beadle (1863-1947), a highly accomplished military artist whose work seems to be all but forgotten today. His finely detailed pencil drawing for the 1917 card is titled "Writing Home," while his 1918 Italian front card is titled "Letters from Home."

Plate 62: 1918 - 6th Canadian Inf. Bde. - Obverse: The 1918 card of the 6th Canadian Infantry Brigade commemorates their successful attack on Rosieres-en-Santerre during the Battle of Amiens. At the outset of their assault they were supported by five tanks of the 14th Tank Battalion, but by the time they reached the village only one remained, shown on the card, and then it too was put out of action during the final onslaught. It took three hours to finally clear the village of its tenacious defenders.

Plate 63: 1918 - 8th Div. - Inside: The 8th Division's card celebrated the Armistice and Christmas with a knock-out in the fourth round. It was printed by Draeger in Paris.

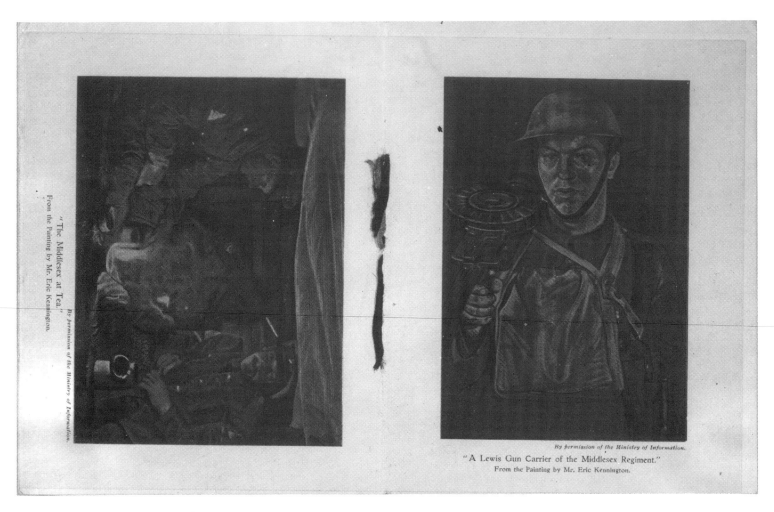

"The Middlesex at Tea."
From the Painting by Mr. Eric Kennington.
By permission of the Ministry of Information.

By permission of the Ministry of Information.
"A Lewis Gun Carrier of the Middlesex Regiment."
From the Painting by Mr. Eric Kennington.

Plate 64: 1918 - 13/Middx. - Inside: During the winter of 1917-1918 Eric Kennington, an official war artist, visited the 13/Middlesex (73rd Brigade, 24th Division) and made these drawings that were then exhibited in London during the summer of 1918.

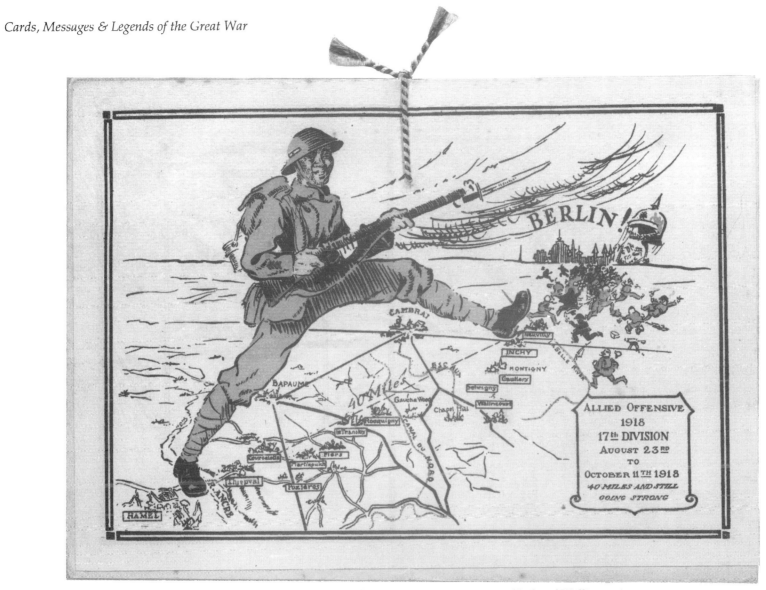

Plate 65: 1918 - 17th Div - Inside: Private W.F.Briggs, 9/Duke of Wellington's West Riding Regiment (52nd Brigade), provided this graphic illustration of the 17th Division's advance from 23rd August to 11th October for their 1918 card. The card was yet another Devambez production.

Plates 66 & 67: 1918 - 2nd Div. - Obverse and *[facing page]* Inside: The design on the obverse of the 2nd Division's 1918 card cleverly incorporated the divisional sign of a red star between two white stars. The gallery of portraits appears on the inside of the card, but nothing is known of the artist, whose monogram was "AK." The card was produced by the Manchester family printing firm Geo. Falkner & Sons. Three of the four Falkner brothers served in the armed forces, including Captain Gilbert E. Falkner, MC, 3/DCLI, who commanded No. 19 Company, MGC.

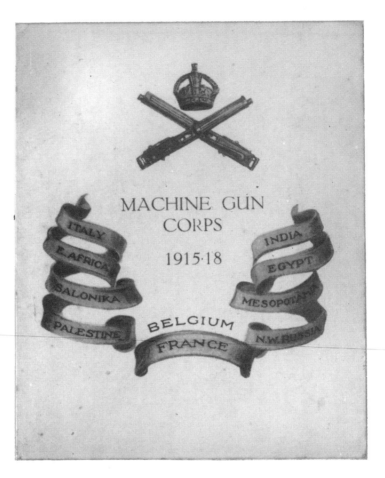

Plates 68 & 69: 1918 - MGC - Obverse & Inside: The Machine Gun Corps 1918 card was an elaborate eight-page colour and black-and-white production to mark the many achievements of its short wartime life. At the peak of its strength the MGC's three branches (cavalry, infantry, motors) mustered a total of 6,427 officers and 123,838 other ranks or, in other words, a force of about the same size as the entire British Regular Army of today. A total of 170,500 officers and men served with the MGC during the war and the Corps suffered 62,049 casualties, including 12,498 dead.

Buckingham Palace. O.H.M.S.

The General Officer Comdg. Machine
Gun Training Centre Grantham.

I have received your telegram
with much pleasure. Please
assure all ranks how proud I am
to be Colonel-in-Chief of the
Machine Gun Corps which has
gained so high a reputation for
efficiency and gallantry in the
field. I shall always follow their
doings with the keenest interest.

18.10.18   George R.I. Colonel-in-Chief.

A Machine Gunner 1918

GREETINGS ⦂⦂
CHRISTMAS 1918 ⟡ NEW YEAR 1919
from

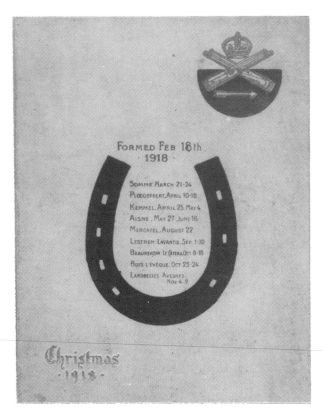

Plate 70: 1918 - 25th Bn. MGC - Obverse: The 25th Battalion, MGC, was formed from the 7th, 74th, 75th and 195th Machine Gun Companies. When the Division was returned to England in June 1918 to be re-formed the battalion remained in France and served with the 59th and 66th Divisions before rejoining the returned 25th Division on 19th October 1918.

Plate 71: 1918 - 19th Div. - Inside: The 19th Division used a butterfly as its sign and this obviously inspired the illustrator and cartoonist W. Heath Robinson (1872-1944) when designing the division's 1918 card.

Christmas 1918

The Huns Retirement according to plan

Plate 72: 1918 - 2nd Cav. Div. - Obverse: During the Final Advance on the Western Front each of the three brigades of the 2nd Cavalry Division was attached to a different Army. For instance, on 11th November the 5th Lancers of its 3rd Cavalry Brigade were with the Canadians of the First Army as they passed through Mons, where the 5th Lancers had fought in 1914.

Plate 73: 1918 - 41st Div. - Inside: The service of the 41st Division on the Italian and Flanders fronts in 1918 was reflected in these drawings in its 1918 card.

Plate 74: 1918 - Lovat's Scouts - Inside: These drawings from their 1918 card chart something of the chequered history of the Lovat's Scouts Yeomanry during the Great War, including, at lower right, their provision of observation sections on the Western Front. These sections were Corps troops and set up special observation posts to keep watch on the enemy front. [See also *Plate 55*]

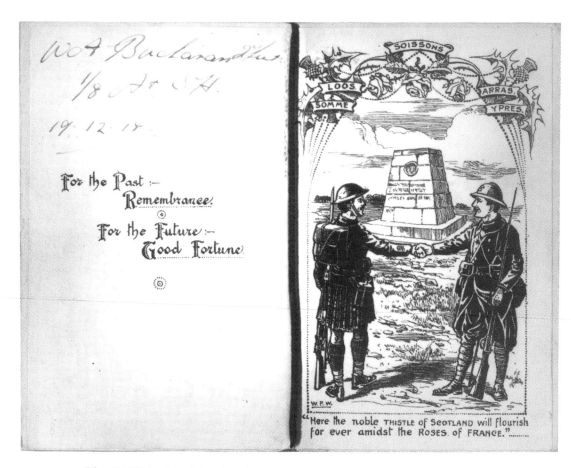

Plate 75: 1918 - 15th Div. - Inside: The 1918 card of the 15th (Scottish) Division included this drawing of their monument at Buzancy, commemorating a joint operation with the French XX Corps on 28th July 1918.